D1387407

brilliant answers

P

PROFILE BOOKS

First published in Great Britain in 2008 by
Profile Books Ltd
3a Exmouth House
Pine Street
Exmouth Market
London EC1R 0JH
www.profilebooks.com

Copyright © IssueBits Ltd 2008

All rights reserved. Without limiting the rights under
copyright reserved above, no part of this publication may
be reproduced, stored or introduced into a retrieval
system, or transmitted, in any form or by any means
(electronic, mechanical, photocopying, recording or
otherwise), without the prior written permission of both
the copyright owner and the publisher of this book.

A CIP catalogue record for this book is available
from the British Library.

ISBN 978 1 84668 216 2

Text design by Sue Lamble
Typeset in Clarendon by MacGuru Ltd
info@macguru.org.uk

Printed and bound in the UK by
CPI Bookmarque, Croydon, CR0 4TD

Answers are provided in good faith by IssueBits Ltd, but
the accuracy of the information in them cannot be
guaranteed by IssueBits or the publisher. No responsibility
for any loss, injury or disappointment arising as a result of
any information provided in this book, accurate or
otherwise, can be accepted by IssueBits or the publisher.
Sure, read about dangerous or daft stuff – just don't try
and do it.

Mixed Sources
Product group from well-managed
forests and other controlled sources
www.fsc.org Cert no. TT-COC-002227
© 1996 Forest Stewardship Council

contents

foreword

Welcome to the wonderful world of AQA 63336. We're that text service where you text any question to 63336 (for £1) and actually get an answer back, in minutes.

If you've read *The End of the Question Mark* (published in 2006) and *Any Question Answered* (published in 2007), you'll know that this is our third book-shaped delve into the AQA 63336 archives. This year we're simply in the realm of *Brilliant Answers*.

A brilliant answer can be a response to a brilliant question – arcane, fiendishly complicated or something that we wished we'd thought of asking ourselves – or it can spring from nowhere, a fact-packed and funny retort to an everyday query.

If someone sensible enough to have our number in their phone asked the title of Sandie Shaw's last UK chart single, the answer would be 'Nothing Less Than Brilliant', which got to number 66 in 1994.

Nobody has asked it yet, but let Sandie's swansong be the theme for the following smorgasbord of essential and non-essential but mightily entertaining information.

Want to be in next year's book? Text 'BOOK' and your question to 63336. If it's picked for the book, we'll send you a special edition AQA 63336 T-shirt.

acknowledgements

Without people, there'd be no questions and no answers. So here's to our customers for texting AQA 63336 with questions – no matter how big or small, easy or difficult. And here's to our wonderful researchers, who come up with all the brilliant answers, in minutes.

food and drink

Brilliance in food and drink depends on context. An exquisitely prepared meal and the finest wines known to humanity are both brilliant. Alternatively, if you were crossing a desert, directions to the nearest well and the faintest hope of a cheese roll would also be pretty splendid. AQA 63336 has helped gourmets and grazers find the food and drink they needed, told them what was in it and warned them off the things that might make them violently ill.

? how many chickens do we eat in our lifetime

In the UK we eat, on average, 1,200 chickens during our lifetime. That's 1,800 kilos of chicken meat, the same as eating a four-year-old elephant.

? do you really lose weight eating celery

Celery takes more calories to consume (more because of digestion than chewing) than it contains. However, you'd need to eat 583 stalks to lose 1lb.

? is a bounty cadburys or nestle

Bounty is made by Mars. When Saddam Hussein was captured, several Bounty bars were found in the fridge of the farmhouse in which he was hiding.

? what are conkers good for

Getting sweets. Each year in Bonn, traffic grinds to a halt as Haribo offers 1kg of sweets for 10kg of conkers, or 5kg of acorns, which go to feed wild boar and deer.

? when was the term lager lout first used

The term 'lager lout' was first used in 1988 by *Sun* journalist Simon Walters, following the Conservative minister John Patten's use of 'lager culture'.

? why is toblerone triangle shaped

Toblerone's shape represents the Matterhorn in the Swiss Alps. It was invented by Theodor Tobler in 1908. *Terrone* is Italian for honey almond nougat.

? how many beers are consumed in the uk every second

On average, 330 pints of beer are consumed per second in the UK. This compares to 448 per second in the Czech Republic, the largest consumer of beer in Europe.

what 10 things cure a hangover

Ten hangover remedies: bananas, water, sugary drinks, pain killers, sleep, fresh air, toast, positive mental attitude, tomato juice, avoiding daytime TV.

how long would it take me to eat a cow

Once an average cow has been butchered, about 800lb of edible meat remains. This would take, at three meals a day, and ½lb meat per meal, six months for you to eat.

which football club has a public house on all four corners of its ground

Brentford's ground, Griffin Park, is famed for having a pub at each corner of the stadium. The best of them is The Griffin, at the southwest corner.

pigs' snouts and sweet larks are what

They are both apples. With over 2,000 varieties of apple in England, you could keep the doctor away by eating a different apple every day for six years.

can you fit an egg into a milk bottle without breaking it

Soak a raw egg in vinegar for two days (it softens the shell). Heat the bottle in boiling water. Place egg on top of the bottle: it will be 'sucked' in.

what product has the barcode 5010024141523

Barcode 5010024141523 is a 500g pack of Saxa coarse sea salt. There's enough salt in the sea to cover Britain to a depth of 50 miles.

? what is the best type of biscuit to make a mattress from

The best type of biscuits to make a mattress from would be fig rolls or strawberry Newtons. They would be soft, but still provide some back support.

? how much food in the uk gets wasted a year

£8bn of food is thrown away annually, which is equivalent to 6.7m tonnes of food. Food accounts for 19% of domestic waste, and fruit is the top item binned.

? is it ok to eat a polar bear's liver

Polar bear liver is toxic to humans because of the extremely high levels of vitamin A. Just 30–90g of vitamin A is enough to kill a person.

❓ why does rhubarb grow faster when deprived of light

Because rhubarb can't photosynthesise in the dark, it puts its energy into producing more brightly coloured and tender shoots, yielding a better harvest.

❓ on average how much time of your life do you spend making cups of tea

The average person drinks 74,802 cups of tea in their lifetime. This equates to around 2,493 hours spent making tea. That's a lot of tea time.

❓ does eating fish really give you brains

Fish contains Omega-3 DHA, which is proven to keep brain cell membranes healthy and appears to aid communication within brain cells. It helps concentration.

? have there always been orange peanut m and ms

No, there have not always been orange peanut M&Ms. Originally, all peanut M&Ms were brown, joined in 1960 by red, green and yellow, then in 1976 by orange.

? does the queen have crusts on cucumber sandwiches at garden parties

At a Buckingham Palace garden party, there are no crusts on cucumber, smoked salmon or asparagus sandwiches. The garden parties cost £500,000 per year.

? abluecrib: an anagram of a beverage

'Abluecrib' is Cuba Libre, a cocktail of cola, lime and rum. It is sometimes known as 'mentirita' (little lie) by Cubans opposed to Castro's government.

? is there such a thing as raspberry lucozade

Raspberry Lucozade exists, as do Tropical, Mixed Citrus, Orange and Caffeine Boost. It was first introduced in 1927 and used in hospitals in 1929.

? where is the uk's biggest freezer

The biggest freezer in the UK, and indeed the world, is at Hams Hall, near Lea Marston, Warwickshire. It can hold up to 1.2 billion fish fingers.

? what is an eastern powder put in food

Prague Powder is a sodium based ingredient used in sausage making. There are two strains known as #1 and #2. It is used to help prevent food poisoning.

? edible plant of the mustard family, used as fodder

Turnip is an edible member of the mustard family which is often grown as animal fodder. The ancient Romans grew turnips for fodder as they grow quickly.

? what is the traditional bird to eat at christmas pre-1950s

In the 1940s, the traditional bird for Christmas dinner was goose. The fat removed during cooking was sometimes made into a chest rub for colds.

? what logical sentence is there with 5 'and's in a row

A sentence with five 'and's in a row is 'When you drew that fish-and-chips sign, you should have put a hyphen between "fish" and "and" and "and" and chips.'

? do lambs have flaps

'Lamb flap' is a cut of meat containing up to 50% fat. It is what we call breast, or belly, of lamb. It is known as 'sipsip' in Papua New Guinea.

? why is a potato called a potato and why is an onion called an onion

'Potato' is derived from the Inca word for sweet potato – *bappa*, which became bappata, then pattata. 'Onion' is from the Latin word *unio*, meaning one.

? where do they get the milk from for baileys

The cream used in Baileys comes from Avonmore Waterford Plc (a co-operative dairy located about 70 miles outside Dublin) and uses 4.3% of Ireland's milk.

❓ the sweets quality street, where is quality street

Quality Street is in Merstham, Surrey. The cul-de-sac inspired a play of the same name, from which the confectioners Mackintosh took the name in 1936.

❓ what year were cadbury cream eggs first sold

Cadbury Creme Eggs were first sold in 1971. The Cadbury Creme Egg plant at Bournville 'lays' 66,000 Creme Eggs every hour, more than 1.5 million a day.

❓ why do people raise their glasses and toast things

The custom of making a toast originated in Ancient Greece, when poisoning was rife. The host would drink first, then raise a glass so others would drink.

? is it true that lettuce has the same effects on rabbits as opium on humans

Yes. Lettuce contains lactucarium, which has an effect similar to opium and has been used in sleeping draughts. It has a soporific effect on rabbits.

? what vegetable can be grown on mars

NASA scientists recently said that the soil on Mars would be good for growing asparagus and turnips, but probably not good enough for strawberries.

? do slugs eat potatoes

Slugs eat 36,000 tonnes of potatoes every year in Britain. The record speed for a slug is 0.2 mph, and slugs can smell a mushroom up to 2 metres away.

what alcohol is used to make a margarita

A Margarita contains 3 parts tequila, 2 parts orange liqueur and 1 part lime juice. The drink is named after Rita Hayworth (real name Margarita Carmen Cansino).

what do shitzu dogs taste like grilled

Shih Tzu dog meat is said to be similar to pork, but with a stronger flavour, a bit like lamb. Poodle meat is said to be quite greasy.

where does the word 'booze' come from

The word 'booze' comes from the Middle Dutch word *busen*, which means 'to drink heavily'. It became 'bouse' in Middle English, and then 'booze'.

the human body

The human body is brilliance in flesh and bone. This triumph of evolutionary research and development is a versatile machine for everything from complex sums to getting the lid off a pickle jar. Of all the organs in the body, the brain is of particular interest to AQA 63336, as that's where brilliant questions and brilliant answers like the following originate.

how many teeth has an adult got in their mouth

Including wisdom teeth, an adult has 32 teeth. A child has 20; dogs have 42. George Washington had dentures made out of hippopotamus teeth.

how many deaths are there every day in the world

There are 1.8 deaths every second; that equates to 155,520 deaths a day. There are 4.1 births every second, which is 354,240 per day.

ever been a fart tax

In 2003 the New Zealand government proposed a methane levy on farmers, but plans were abandoned after fierce criticism that labelled it a 'fart tax'.

how much human blood can you buy for £5

For £5, you can buy 20ml of human blood. For £102, you can buy 500ml of human blood. It is, millilitre for millilitre, half the price of printer ink.

? what do you call the phobia of little holes like those found in sponges and honeycomb and crumpets

'Trypophobia' is the name given to a fear of holes. This includes human pores and holes in cheese, rocks, coral, sponges, ice, honeycomb and crumpets.

? what day of the week has the highest percentage of heart attacks

Monday is the most dangerous day of the week for heart attacks, with 20% more occurring. This is to do with the stress of work.

? what's the largest tumour

The largest tumour ever recorded was an ovarian cyst weighing 328lb (23.4 stone) removed from a woman in Texas in 1905. The patient recovered.

can you get drunk off pee

Only 5–10% of alcohol drunk is excreted unchanged in urine, breath and sweat. This isn't enough to get drunk, even from the urine of a heavy drinker.

how far do you sneeze

The spray radius of a sneeze is 15 feet. It is a reflex response using the muscles of the face, throat and chest, releasing up to 40,000 droplets.

i am having ass problems

AQA is sorry to hear you're having ass problems; you could try some donkey obedience training. AQA hears that the carrot and stick method works well.

how much hair do men lose every day

Men lose 500–1000 strands of hair a day, and follicles grow new hair in their place. This stops when you reach the late teens, and you then begin to go bald due to higher levels of testosterone.

how much do you get paid to donate sperm

When donating sperm, you can claim loss of earnings up to a daily maximum of £55.19. This is capped at £250 per course of sperm donation.

what is the organ associated with scary things called

The kidney is the organ associated with fear. The liver is associated with anger, the lungs with sadness, the heart with joy, and the spleen with worry.

what is the only bone in your body not attached to anything

The hyoid bone, just above the larynx, anchors the muscles of the tongue and is the only bone in the body that doesn't touch any other bone.

? does a smoker pay more in tax than they receive in health care

Yes. While an average smoker costs the NHS £150 a year, they pay £949 each year in tax – six times more.

? what natural anti-dandruff shampoos are there

Rinse your hair with ordinary vinegar or lemon juice before washing it. Also make sure you live somewhere where it constantly snows, thus disguising the problem.

? is there anything i can do to make my penis bigger

There is no natural way of enlarging your penis. Many pills and operations which claim to do so are dubious and risky. 45% of men want a bigger penis.

? why is one lung smaller than the other in the human body

In human bodies, the right lung is larger and heavier than the left lung, due to the position of the heart. The right lung takes in more air.

? what's the lowest calorie alcohol i can drink

Vodka is the least calorific drink: one shot with Diet Coke is only 50 calories. The lowest calorie beer is Michelob Ultra at 95 calories per bottle.

? give me a good excuse for taking an afternoon nap

Research suggests that an afternoon nap as short as 10 minutes can enhance alertness, mood and mental performance, especially after a night of poor sleep.

what should i call my boyfriend's penis

Boost his ego by calling it Mr Big Boy. Over 70% of men and 64% of women have a pet name for their genitalia. Macaulay Culkin named his penis 'Floyd'.

is kissing bad for you

Kissing is not bad for you, as it stimulates the flow of saliva, which helps to reduce plaque levels. It is nature's most enjoyable cleaning process.

when was the first case of cancer registered and where

Cancer was first described in Egypt in 1600 BC. The 'Father of Medicine', the Greek physician Hippocrates (460–370 BC), first used the word *carcinos* (cancer).

wot is bermuda blaming its obesity on

Jennifer Attride-Stirling, health coordinator of Bermuda, blamed Bermuda's rise in the world obesity table on too many 'massive bowls of Coco Pops'.

what is the smallest birth weight ever recorded for a baby

Rumaisa Rahman holds the record for the smallest birthweight baby to survive. Born at 25 weeks gestation in 2004, she weighed just 8.6oz.

what is the world record for hiccups

Charles Osborne, an Iowan farmer, entered the *Guinness Book of World Records* as the man with the longest attack of hiccups lasting from 1922 to 1990, a total of 68 years.

is it true that pregnant women are said to have a glow about them or look well

The pregnancy 'glow' does have a biological basis: increases in blood volume and oil secretion during pregnancy give the skin a healthy blush and shine.

❓ why when breaking wind is it sometimes loud and sometimes quiet

The noise made by breaking wind is the vibration of the anal sphincter. The factors which alter the volume are sphincter tightness, gas volume and speed.

❓ what is the longest muscle name in the human body

The 'musculus levator labii superioris alaeque nasi' is the muscle with the longest name. It's the muscle Elvis used to create his trademark lip curl.

❓ what is the etymology of the phrase, to have 'blue blood' – why blue for the aristocracy

Blue blood comes from the Spanish *sangre azul*. Wealthy Castilian families claiming to be pure bred would point to their prominent blue veins.

how many people die every second

1.7 people die every second. The odds of a meteorite crashing on your house and killing you are 182 trillion to 1. Dying in a car crash is 18,585 to 1.

what percentage of bone is water

Bone is 22% water. There are 206 bones in an adult body. 82% of blood, 70% of the brain and 90% of the lungs is water. Jellyfish are 95% water.

how much does your tummy expand when you have eaten

The stomach rests at a volume of 75ml, but after eating it can expand to 2l, or 26.6 times its normal size. It is controlled by the P2Y1 and P2Y11 proteins.

? how much horse power can the average human generate

A healthy human can produce about 1.2 hp briefly, and sustain about 0.1 hp indefinitely. An athlete can manage up to 0.3 hp for a sustained period.

? how long does it take to incinerate a human body

It takes 2½ hours to cremate an average person at 1000°C. The dried bone fragments are then put into a cremulator, which pulverises them, creating 'ashes'.

? what is rumpology

Rumpology is divination (fortune-telling) by reading the lines and crevices of a person's buttocks. It's like getting your palm read, only more personal.

the big and
small screens

Not all films and television programmes are
brilliant, but all can make for brilliant answers.
It's even possible to winkle out stunning, startling
facts about monumental clunkers like Ishtar and
Eldorado. In this section, AQA 63336 celebrates the
legends of Hollywood, Pinewood and Wood Lane,
London W12 8QT.

? **i want to write a film script, which makes me millions, what should it be about**

Based on the top-grossing films, your script should be about a young wizard and a robot looking for a ring on a pirate ship which sinks. Good luck.

? **what two words were a book, an oscar winning film and a singer**

Tom Jones is an Oscar-winning film (1963), a book (written by Henry Fielding) and a singer. It is also the name of two operas and a professional golfer.

? **how long would it take aqa to find out how many times the phrase 'declaration of independence' is used in the film national treasure**

About 38 seconds. The phrase 'Declaration of Independence' is spoken 22 times in the film *National Treasure*. The document contained a clue to hidden treasure.

❓ how many dvds does the average person own in britain

Britons own 76 DVDs on average, watching their favourites around 22 times. 68% of Britons would rather wait for DVD releases than watch films at the cinema.

❓ how long would it take jack bauer to get off the lost island

Jack Bauer would be able to get off the *Lost* island in about 24 hours. For some unknown reason, everything Jack does seems to take this long.

❓ what is the combined running time of all the rambo films

The four 'Rambo' films have a combined running time of 382 minutes. In the films, Rambo has killed a total of 415 people, or one person every 55 seconds.

who was the bond girl that was a man

Caroline 'Tula' Cossey appeared as an extra in the 1981 Bond film *For Your Eyes Only*. She was born Barry Kenneth Cossey, and had a sex change in 1974.

which film director won two of the top american medals for his role as a soldier in the vietnam war

Film director Oliver Stone was awarded the Bronze Star and the Purple Heart during his time as a soldier in the Vietnam war. He directed *Platoon*.

how many cigarettes does humphrey bogart smoke on screen in the film casablanca

Humphrey Bogart smoked thirteen cigarettes in the film *Casablanca*. No female character smokes in the film; their cigarettes are held, but never lit.

who played the tin man in wizard of oz

Jack Haley played the Tin Man in *The Wizard of Oz*. His son, Jack Jr, married Liza Minnelli. Minnelli's mother, Judy Garland, played Dorothy in the film.

what actress was penelope pitstop based on

Penelope Pitstop was based on the character Maggie DuBois from *The Great Race* (1965), the film that inspired Wacky Races. DuBois was played by Natalie Wood.

what school did captain hook supposedly go to

Captain Hook went to Eton. J. M. Barrie hinted at this in *Peter Pan* and confirmed it in a speech at Eton College in 1927, entitled 'Captain Hook at Eton'.

how long before someone talks in the movie 2001 a space odyssey

The first line in *2001: A Space Odyssey* (1968) is spoken 25 minutes and 38 seconds into the film. The line is 'Here you are, sir. Main level, please.'

in the film 300 what is the body count of people killed

The official body count in Zack Snyder's 2006 film *300* was 585. The word 'Sparta' is used 72 times in total during the film, or 0.62 times per minute.

what is the longest film in the world

The longest film ever made is the somewhat aptly titled *Cure for Insomnia* (1987), which has a duration of 87 hours. It features L. D. Groban reading a poem.

? which three films have been remade the most times – ie the most adaptations

> *A Christmas Carol* is the most remade film, with over 60 versions, closely followed by *Frankenstein* (51 versions) and *Dracula* (43 versions).

? what was princess leia's cell number in star wars iv

> In *Star Wars Episode IV: A New Hope*, Princess Leia's cell number is 2187. The cell block is 1138. These numbers are both in the titles of films George Lucas made as a student.

? on top gear, what car did james use to race a pigeon

> In *Top Gear*, James May drove a Ford SportKa when he raced a homing pigeon. James had a navigation system and the pigeon had a top speed of 70 mph. The pigeon won easily.

? what sort of car did dangermouse drive

Dangermouse drove the Mark III car – a masterpiece of engineering. It had telescopically extending wings and an onboard videophone, and could drive up walls.

? where is the fairground in the lost boys

The fairground in the 1987 film *The Lost Boys* is on Santa Cruz Boardwalk in California. Parts of the 1983 film *Sudden Impact* were also filmed there.

? what was the first film sequel that had 2 as a suffix

Quatermass 2 was the first film sequel to have the suffix '2'. The film was released in 1957. In America it is known as *Enemy From Space*.

? how long would it take to watch all the star trek episodes ever made including the animated ones

It would take 22 days, 16 hours and 2 minutes to watch all 726 episodes of the 6 *Star Trek* TV series. 30 seasons of *Star Trek* have been made.

? why do telephone numbers in american films invariably contain the sequence 555

In the 1970s, US phone companies asked films and TV to use the prefix 555 to avoid confusion with real numbers. The Simpsons' phone number is 555–0113.

? what colour was the cornetto in hot fuzz

The white Cornetto Classico appears in *Hot Fuzz*. *Shaun of the Dead* features Cornetto Strawberry. Cornetto Mint will appear in 'The World's End' (working title).

? what's the longest running tv soap in the uk

> *Coronation Street* is the longest running TV soap opera in the UK. It was first broadcast in 1960. It was created by scriptwriter Tony Warren.

? were real spiders used in the film arachnophobia

> 374 real spiders (Delena cancerides) were used in the 1990 film *Arachnophobia* – they are harmless to humans. The giant spider was an articulated model.

? could you text me an embarrassing fact about malta

> Malta has never won the Eurovision Song Contest. Despite this, 90% of the population of Malta watch the contest on television every year.

when was the 1st tv advert broadcast in the uk

The first TV advert broadcast in the UK was on ITV on 22 September 1955. It promoted Gibbs SR toothpaste, claiming, 'It's tingling fresh. It's fresh as ice.'

name 5 british tv shows that have green in the title

The Green Green Grass (BBC), *Tales From the Green Valley* (BBC), *It's Not Easy Being Green* (BBC2), *Green Wing* (C4) and *Camberwick Green* (BBC1).

what's the longest advert ever made

The longest advert ever recorded was for Emirates Airlines in 2007. Brazilian Fernando Ferreira speaks for 14 hours and 14 minutes about his home city of São Paulo.

? **what is the movie connection between viv richards, guy gibson, the matrix reloaded, zoe slater, eggs benedict, richard kimble and dennis quaid**

> Arnold Schwarzenegger played characters called Richards, Gibson, Benedict, Matrix, Kimble, Slater and Quaid. The riddle could also ask about sugar 'Cane'.

? **what film holds the record for the most use of fake blood**

> Peter Jackson's *Braindead* used a record 300l of fake blood in its final scene alone. Fake blood is made of syrup, water and food colouring.

famous people

To be brilliant is to shine. Stars shine. Ergo, all stars are brilliant, even the rubbish Z-list ones. In the interests of diplomacy, AQA 63336 would like to make it clear that the following brilliant answers concern only the greatest ladies, gentlemen and animals ever to achieve fame. Honest.

where was jerry springer born

Jerry Springer was born in East Finchley tube station, London, in 1944. His parents, Margot and Richard Springer, were Jewish refugees from Nazi Germany.

what was diana dors's chest size

Diana Dors's bust measured 36.5D. Born Diana Mary Fluck, she said her name was changed in case it was put up in lights and one of the theatre lights blew.

how tall is jeremy clarkson

Jeremy Clarkson is 6ft 5in tall. He began presenting *Top Gear* in 1988. His mother made a fortune from manufacturing Paddington Bear merchandise.

who got more fan mail than the beatles

Adolf Hitler received more fan mail during the 1930s and 1940s than The Beatles, The Rolling Stones and Madonna have since received combined.

what was arnold scharzenegger's first ever film

Arnold Schwarzenegger's first film role (as Arnold Strong) was as Hercules in *Hercules in New York*. His accent was so bad they had to dub all of his lines.

what illness did david niven die of

David Niven died in Switzerland on 29 July 1983 of motor neurone disease, aged 73. Raymond Massey, his co-star in *Prisoner of Zenda*, died the same day.

how old is russell brand please

Russell Brand is 33 years old. The comedian collected the GQ award for Most Stylish Man in 2006, and the award for Least Stylish Man in 2007.

scooby doo, fowler, four weddings and a funeral, beans what is the connection

Rowan Atkinson is the link between Scooby Doo (in the 2002 film), Fowler (*The Thin Blue Line*), *Four Weddings & a Funeral* (in the film) and beans (Mr Bean).

which comedian was a prison warden for rudolf hess

Bernard Manning guarded Nazi war criminals Rudolf Hess, Albert Speer and Karl Doenitz at Spandau Prison, Berlin. The prison was demolished in 1987.

who says never use yellow lipstick

'Never wear yellow lipstick' is one of the essential beauty rules of Miss Piggy from *The Muppets*. She also cautions against powdering your tongue.

who is the most portrayed character in film

Sherlock Holmes is the most portrayed character on film, and has been played by 72 different actors in 204 films. Basil Rathbone played Holmes 14 times.

was danny baker responsible for the death of bob marley

No. Danny Baker broke Bob Marley's toe in a 1977 football match, and Marley's cancer began with a foot melanoma, but the game was after the onset of illness.

? **which native american
indian was buried in london
in the 19th century**

> Chief Long Wolf, part of Buffalo Bill's
> Wild West Show, died of pneumonia
> and was buried in London in 1892.
> His body was returned to South
> Dakota in 1997.

? **what did neil armstrong say
next**

> After his 'one small step' speech, Neil
> Armstrong continued: 'Yes, the
> surface is fine and powdery. I can kick
> it up loosely with my toe.'

? **why does alan hansen off tv
have a scar on his head**

> Alan Hansen got the scar on his head
> as a result of running through a glass
> door when he was 17. He had 27
> stitches and was in hospital for four
> hours.

who was the first female london bus driver

Jill Viner was the first female bus driver for London Transport. Her first route was the 65 between Chessington and Ealing on 6 May 1974. She died in 1996.

when did kerry katona marry mark croft

Kerry Katona married cab driver Mark Croft at Gretna Green on 14 February 2007. Runaway marriages have been performed in the village since 1753.

which tattooed female singer does not have a television in her house

Amy Winehouse does not have a television in her house. She is also a fussy eater, only consuming foods such as KFC, tuna salad and chicken soup.

? **did robert de niro play the lion in any wizard of oz play or film**

When Robert de Niro was 10 years old, he portrayed the Cowardly Lion in a local production of *The Wizard of Oz*. He has starred in over fifty films.

? **what is lady helen guest better known as**

The actress Jamie Lee Curtis can be known as Baroness Haden-Guest, or Lady Haden-Guest. Her husband, Christopher, created the film *This Is Spinal Tap*.

? **who was the last man on the moon**

The last man on the moon was Eugene Cernan of the Apollo 17 mission. This was in December 1972, 3 years and 5 months after Neil Armstrong first stood on the moon.

❓ who is britain's vainest man

Scott Alexander, a personal trainer and self-made millionaire, is Britain's vainest man. He takes three hours to get ready and spends £500k a year on cosmetics.

❓ what president said how can a president not be an actor

When asked 'How can an actor become president?' Ronald Reagan replied, 'How can a president not be an actor?' He also said 'Getting shot hurts.'

❓ which snooker player famously farted during a major tournament

Bill Werbeniuk famously farted at the Crucible and then said 'Who did that?' A heavy drinker, he managed to claim lager as an overhead for tax purposes.

who was the first ever snowboarder

Sherman Poppen is considered to be the first ever snowboarder. In 1965, he invented the Snurfer (two skis bound together) as a toy for his daughter.

who was the first serial killer

Liu Pengli, cousin of Emperor Jing of China, is history's first serial killer. Operating at night from around 144 to 121 BC, he murdered over 100 people.

which art school did salvador dali go to

Salvador Dali studied at the Academia de San Fernando in Madrid. He was expelled after claiming no one there was competent enough to judge his work.

? what links london zoo and singapore

Sir Thomas Stamford Raffles links London Zoo and Singapore. The colonial official established London Zoo in 1826 after founding Singapore in 1819.

? what did thomas edison invent

Thomas Edison invented the phonograph, kinetoscope, dictaphone, radio, electric lamp, autographic printer and tattoo gun. His middle name was Alva.

? who was henry viii's mother

Henry VIII was the second son of Elizabeth of York and Henry VII. The picture of the queen found in a deck of cards is based on Elizabeth's image.

? which british actress starred in a jelly tots advert age three

Sadie Frost appeared in a Jelly Tots advert aged 3. She also appeared on *The Morecambe and Wise Show* aged 5. She was born in Primrose Hill, London.

? what's thatcher's relationship to ice cream

Margaret Thatcher was part of a science team which invented soft ice cream, a process that involved putting more air in the product, thus reducing ingredients and costs.

? did rowan atkinson land a plane

Rowan Atkinson hasn't landed a plane, but he briefly took charge of a small aircraft when its pilot collapsed at the controls. The pilot came round.

? who was first choice actor ahead of j travolta to play vincent vaga in pulp fiction

John Travolta was the first choice for Vincent Vega in *Pulp Fiction*. Daniel Day Lewis wanted the role, but Quentin Tarantino turned him down.

? what was the name of the hangman who hung dick turpin

Thomas Hadfield hanged Dick Turpin. He was once Turpin's friend and fellow gang member, but was pardoned because he agreed to be the hangman.

? what do bob marley and jack daniels have in common

A big toe killed both Bob Marley in 1981 and Jack Daniel in 1911. Marley died of cancer and Daniel of blood poisoning, both originating in their toes.

who created playdough

Play-Doh was invented by Noah and Joseph McVicker in 1956 and awarded US Patent 3,167,440 in 1965. It was originally designed as a wallpaper cleaner.

how old is katie white

Katie White, the female lead singer of the Ting Tings, is 25. In Japan, where the band are very popular, their name means 'small, cute penis'.

what is the full name for charlie oatway, the brighton football player

Charlie Oatway's full name is Anthony Philip David Terry Frank Donald Stanley Gerry Gordon Stephen James Oatway. He was named after QPR's 1973 first team.

5

from celebrities

As the previous chapter suggests, AQA 63336 maintains sizable dossiers on most bods in the public eye. Sometimes, however, the most brilliant answers to celebrity questions can come only from the celebrities themselves.

robbie keane, footballer

? what is more important in making a top grade footballer, talent or application

They are both vital ingredients and one on its own really isn't enough. For me, you need that, enthusiasm and a real love of playing football.

? does the noise of the crowd really affect the players

It can when you allow it to. If there is a real buzz in the ground you can be inspired by it and use the atmosphere to your advantage – particularly at home. When the crowd are against you at an away game you can shut it out.

? if you could play in the same team as any other player past or present who would it be

I think it would have to be Zidane.

stuart broad,
england cricketer

**? what's the most memorable
wicket you've taken**

> My dad – when I was at school. He
> was playing for the MCC against the
> school first XI. I got him for LBW. A
> bit fortuitous, but it was all about the
> appeal.

**? who was your boyhood
cricketing hero**

> Glenn McGrath. He's been a model
> professional throughout his career. I
> admire his skill, he's exciting to
> watch and got me interested in
> bowling at an early age. There's no
> better role model for someone like me.

what's the best bit of advice someone's ever given you

It came from my mum, when I was 14 or 15. I remind myself of it every day: Make sure you put your heart and soul into whatever you do. When you do this, results and performance come with it. Play and do everything with a smile on your face.

what advice would you give to young cricketers eager to get to your level

Keep it simple, enjoy your sport, play for the level of the game. Cricket is still a hobby for me – I enjoy a Saturday game, a test... Just let your natural ability and hard work take you where you want to be.

tiff needell, *5th gear* tv presenter

? what is your favourite car

The McLaren F1 Supercar put the biggest smile on my face. Only 107 have ever been produced, it has a top speed of 242 mph, and in one I hold the official lap record for a UK circuit in a production car at an average of 195.3 mph.

? who's your boyhood hero

Jim Clark, the Scottish Grand Prix star and greatest driver ever! He won two world championships and also the Indianapolis 500 once back in the 1960s.

? what's the best movie driving scene

It's in the 1971 film *The Burglars* (also known as *Le Casse*). It has the wildest, no tricks, genuine stunt driving chase ever made.

? **what car would you most
like to smash up**

> Every G Wiz electric car ever made –
> they are a danger to anyone who
> thinks it's a clever idea to get in one.

jean-christophe novelli, chef

? what's the best way to cook an omelette

Omelette pan, get nice and hot, teaspoon of oil, knob of butter, mix 2–3 eggs thoroughly, season with salt/pepper, pour mix into hot pan, keep folding through, moving the pan, until starting to set on bottom of pan, fold in third and turn out on to a plate.

? who would win a fight between keith floyd and rick stein

I have to say Keith, as he is my friend and mentor, but don't tell Rick!

? if you had to choose, would you rather be good in the kitchen, or good in bed

Luckily for me I don't have to choose.

? what's the best piece of advice you've ever been given

Always confit garlic before using it, as this removes the acid and mellows the bitter taste.

judge jules, radio 1 dj

? **what question would you most like aqa 63336 to answer for you**

> I've spent about a million quid texting you in the middle of the night, so I've run out of questions.

? **if you could take 3 tracks to a desert island, what would they be**

> Raze, 'Break for Love'; Massive Attack, 'Safe from Harm'; and PVD 'Love Stimulation'.

? **who would win a fight between norman cook and pete tong and why**

> Jeez, now you're asking. If sobriety makes you a better fighter and the fight took place during clubbing hours, then Pete Tong, I guess.

? what's the meaning of life

Treating others as you expect to be
treated yourself, with mutual respect
and understanding.

susan quilliam,
agony aunt

**how long should you wait
before texting someone
after the first date**

> Generally, text the next day and
> definitely before lunchtime. Women
> will start worrying after a date if they
> haven't received anything during the
> morning.

**should i end a text with x's,
and if so, how many**

> Count the kisses. One's courteous,
> two's friendly, three states an
> intention. If you're head over heels,
> send a whole screenful to make it
> clear!

**when is it good to text after
a drunken snog**

> You should text the next day, but not
> before lunchtime. You need to wait
> until the hangover disappears before
> making contact.

? when is it better not to text

Some things, actually, are better done face to face. Divorcing should never be done by text (Britney take note). And proposals of marriage should always be done when you can look into someone's eyes and hold their hand.

6

sporting endeavours

Sport, claimed the Bonzo Dog Doo-Dah Band, equips a young man for society. In reality, dedicated sports players usually have to be antisocial in their pursuit of brilliance, which is often achieved at great personal sacrifice. They do, however, have it cushy compared with the ancient Mayans …

which british football club has no letters from the word 'football' in its name

Dundee is the only British football club that has no letters from the word 'football' in its name. Founded in 1893, Dundee play at Dens Park.

did the ancient mayans invent a lethal ball game

The Mayans' ball game, called Tlachtlic, sometimes ended in a human sacrifice. They invented latex, which they used to make the rubber balls.

can you tell an obscure use for vaseline

Boxers use Vaseline during fights to treat bleeding cuts. The inventor, Robert Chesebrough, ate a spoonful every day. AQA does not recommend trying this.

? **has a professional football manager ever been sacked during a game**

> Yes, in 1999 Harald Schumacher (the former West German goalkeeper) was fired at half time with his team Fortuna Cologne trailing 2–0 to Waldhof Mannheim.

? **if u play someone at golf for twelve pence a hole double or quits and win every one how much are u owed**

> If you win 18 holes in a double-or-quits match with a starting bet of 12p, you would win £15,728.64. You would also be buying the drinks at the 19th hole.

? **what came first in football linesmen, shirt numbers or world cup**

> Linesmen, introduced in 1891, came first. The first World Cup was won by Uruguay in 1930, and shirt numbers were compulsory in league matches from 1939.

? how many ski resorts are there in the world

There are 5,758 ski resorts in the world including 17 in Iran, 19 in New York and 3 in England. Skiing is said to have been invented by the goddess Skadi.

? what sport has a coffin, bomb and priest in

American football has a coffin, bomb and priest. A bomb is a long forward pass, a coffin is a corner by the end zone, and Priest Holmes is the name of a player.

? which three wimbledon male champions from 1950 to 2000 were born in germany

John McEnroe, Boris Becker and Michael Stich are the three male Wimbledon champions from 1950 to 2000 who were born in Germany.

? what is the fastest scalextric car

The fastest analogue Scalextric car is the Scalextric MG Lola. It travels at 3.1 mph. This is the same as a full size version travelling at 221.5 mph.

? which football teams have won the fa cup the most, north or south

Manchester United have won the most FA Cups with 11. Northern (north of Watford) teams have won 84; southern teams have won 43. Wanderers won it first.

? what's the oldest game in the world

Backgammon is the oldest game in the world, and archaeologists have found backgammon sets that date from 3000 BC. The doubling cube was added in 1926.

? which football player has never missed a penalty in his career

Ipswich Town's Tommy Miller has never missed a penalty kick in his career. He has scored 24, his first being for Hartlepool, at Mansfield, in 1999.

? what's the connection between man utd, lancashire, vivaldi and mars

Red. Manchester United are the Red Devils, Mars is the Red Planet, Vivaldi was *Il Prete Rosso* (The Red Priest) and Lancashire's symbol is the red rose.

? who was the swedish footballer who played for arsenal and fiorentina who had it in his contract that he couldn't go into space

When former Arsenal and Fiorentina midfielder Stefan Schwarz joined Sunderland in 1999, he had a clause in his contract that banned him from space travel.

? what is the highest win in a game of poker

The highest win in a single game of poker is held by Andy Beal. He won $10.6 million playing Texas Hold 'Em in May 2004 at the Bellagio in Las Vegas.

? has any footballer worn number 69 on his shirt

Bixente Lizarazu wore shirt number 69 at Bayern Munich in 2005/6. His explanation was that he was born in 1969, his height was 1.69m and he weighed 69kg.

? which english army officer issued footballs to his men to go over the top with in 1916

Captain W. P. Nevill was the English army officer who issued footballs to his men for them to play in no man's land on 1 July 1916.

who was the chinese man that played football for england

Capped nine times between 1942 and 1945, Frank Soo is the only player of oriental descent to play for England. He later managed the Israeli national side.

who was the first player in rugby union to play for two different countries in two different world cups

Frank Bunce was the first man to play for two different countries in the Rugby World Cup. He represented Western Samoa in 1991 and New Zealand in 1995.

how many times was michael schumacher out-qualified during his career

Michael Schumacher was out-qualified in 133 Grand Prix. He secured pole position for a record 68 of his 201 total Grand Prix starts. That's 33.8%.

? has any driver won their first race in their first season in formula one

The Italian driver Giancarlo Baghetti is the only driver to win a debut race in F1, at Reims in 1961. Lewis Hamilton came third in his first F1 race.

? how many favourites have won the grand national

The Grand National has been won by the favourite 27 times since the first race in 1836. Four horses have won at odds of 100/1. Only two horses finished in 1928.

? which sport keeps you the fittest – running, cycling or swimming

Swimming keeps you fitter, as it works almost all the muscle groups in the body, whereas runners and cyclists predominantly work their legs.

how many events were there at the montreal olympics

There were 198 events in 23 sports in the 1976 Montreal Olympics. It was the only time in history where the host country failed to win any gold medals.

how long is someone out of football if they break both bones in their leg

The normal recovery period for fractured bones is between three and four months. Different fitness levels and the healing process may mean not playing for over six months.

from 1986 have england ever won a penalty shoot-out in international football

Since 1986, England have had seven penalty shoot-outs. They have won once, against Spain at Wembley in 1996. In shoot-outs they have taken 36 penalties and scored 24.

? what 2 players scored for both teams in an fa cup final

Three players have scored for both teams in an FA Cup final: Bert Turner (Charlton, 1946), Tommy Hutchison (Man City, 1981) and Gary Mabbutt (Spurs, 1987).

? what english football team has a name that starts with 5 consonants

Crystal Palace is the only league football club in England whose name begins with five consonants. Palace's nicknames include The Glaziers and The Eagles.

? who are the only 2 managers to have managed 4 different premier league teams

Graeme Souness (Liverpool, Blackburn, Southampton and Newcastle) and Ron Atkinson (Nottingham Forest, Coventry, Sheffield Wednesday and Aston Villa) have each managed four clubs.

? name 12 countries scotland has a 100% record against

> Scotland have a 100% record against Bosnia and Herzegovina, Cyprus, Iceland, Israel, Latvia, San Marino, Canada, Trinidad and Tobago, Chile, Ecuador, Hong Kong and CIS.

? has any team other than england in 2007 reached the rugby world cup final after losing a group match

> England's loss in 1991 to New Zealand was the only other time that a WC finalist was beaten in the group stages of the competition. France drew in 1987.

? how many 18-hole golf courses are in the uk

> The UK has 2,758 18-hole golf courses. There are 31,548 worldwide, 59% of which are in North America. There are 57,000,000 golfers worldwide.

what is the record for goals scored by one team in an fa cup game

Preston North End have scored the most goals ever in an FA Cup match. In October 1887, they beat Hyde FC 26–0 in the first round of the prestigious cup.

what is the smallest town in france to have had a top flight football club

The smallest town in France to have hosted a top flight club is Guingamp, population 8,008. The club EA Guingamp have played in France's Ligue 1.

why is astroturf called astroturf

AstroTurf is so called because it was first used in the Houston Astrodome in Texas. It was originally called Chemgrass, and was invented in 1964.

? **what was the first car manufacturer to win a formula one race**

> Alfa Romeo, in 1950, was the first car manufacturer to win a F1 race. Alfa Romeo went on to dominate the early years of the sport.

? **game played with top and string – these are the letters that i have d-a-o-o**

> The game played with a spinning top and string that you are looking for is 'Diabolo'. Diabolo has been played in China for 4,000 years.

? **eleven players take the plunge: 4–4**

> The football team in question is Team Bath. The club was founded in 1999, and in 2002 became the first university team to enter the FA Cup since 1881.

**? which nation of the world
are the biggest gamblers**

> Hong Kong is the nation with the
> biggest gamblers – over 5% of the
> adult population are problem
> gamblers, whereas in the UK this
> figure is just 0.6%.

**? what's the most people that
have been sent off in one
game in the world**

> In a league match between Sportivo
> Ameliano and General Caballero in
> Paraguay, 20 players were dismissed
> after fighting broke out. The match
> was abandoned.

**? which countries have taken
part in every summer and
winter olympics**

> Only three countries have participated
> in all 25 summer Olympics (since
> 1896) and all 20 winter Olympics
> (since 1924): Great Britain, France
> and Switzerland.

longest point in tennis

The longest-ever singles tennis point, or rally, was 643 shots, between Jean Hepner and Vicky Nelson in a tournament in Richmond, USA, in October 1984.

name some comedy animals or inanimate objects usain bolt is quicker than

At 23.02 mph Usain Bolt is faster than Roadrunner, who reached a top speed of 15 mph, and Speedy Gonzales, at 8 mph. He is not as quick as Sonic the Hedgehog, at 760 mph.

who was the bravest olympian

Shun Fujimoto helped Japan win gymnastics team gold in the 1976 Olympics, despite a broken knee. Asked if he'd do it again, he replied, 'No, I would not.'

music, lyrics and language

Brilliance looms large in music and literature. Before forming the KLF, Jimmy Cauty was in a band called Brilliant. Brilliant they might have been, successful they weren't. *My Brilliant Career* by Australian novelist Miles Franklin has done rather better since it was first published in 1901. In this chapter, we answer questions on creative excellence in our own excellently brilliant way.

? what connects delia to rolling stones

> The Rolling Stones released their album *Let It Bleed* in 1969, with a cake on the cover. The cake was made by Delia Smith, then an unknown cookery writer.

? i'm 27 and a music fan: what is the approx amount of songs i've heard in my life

> At 27, you have spent a full five years of your life listening to 800,000 songs. The bad news is that six weeks of this was Celine Dion.

? how many languages are there in the world and is there anyone who can speak them all

> There are 6,809 languages spoken in the world. Nobody can speak them all, but Giuseppe Mezzofanti spoke over 38 and was the greatest linguist of all time.

hello there: what is the longest word you can write without using the same letter twice x

At 17 letters, subdermatoglyphic is the longest isogram – a word you can write without using the same letter twice. There are three 15-letter isograms.

what skin are scottish bagpipes made of

Traditionally, pipe bags were made of sheep leather, made airtight by treating with honey. Today's bags are made from Gore-Tex and treated with sealant.

what is the world's funniest word

The funniest word in the English language is fartlek (an athletic training regime); other funny words include furphy, pratfall, parp and firkin.

? who sang the song bicycle race

> 'Bicycle Race' was sung by the group Queen. The video for the song featured a bicycle race with 65 naked girls on bikes borrowed from Halfords.

? what is the name for a victory where you lose more than you gain

> A Pyrrhic victory is one which costs the victor a great deal. It is an allusion to King Pyrrhus of Epirus, whose army suffered mass casualties in a war.

? who is the biggest selling live music artist of all time out of all genres of music

> Michael Jackson is the biggest selling artist still alive, having sold over 100 million albums. The 1983 *Thriller* album sold 50 million copies alone.

? what pop group did ricky jervais star in

Ricky Gervais was in a largely unsuccessful 1980s pop band called Seona Dancing, and also managed Suede in the early 1990s before they were signed.

? what's the most featured song in films of all time

The song most featured in films is 'Happy Birthday to You'. It was written as a classroom greeting in 1893 by two Louisville teachers.

? has classical music ever prevented vandalism

Yes, in 2003, the statue of Isambard Kingdom Brunel, in Swindon town centre, was saved from further vandalism by a protective field of classical music.

what did the beatles contribute to medical research

The CT scanner, invented in 1971, is said to be the 'greatest legacy' of The Beatles; huge profits from their record sales enabled EMI to fund the necessary research.

how many ipods would i need to store the estimated amount of original released songs in the world

With 4 billion original released songs in the world, you'd need 4 million 4GB iPod Nanos, or 100,000 of the new 160GB iPod Classics to store them.

is pete doherty famous for poetry

Pete Doherty has never won any major awards, but at 16 he won a competition and was chosen to travel with the British Council to Russia to perform his poetry.

? which metal band caused stickers to be put on cds

It was Prince, not a metal band, who inspired Parental Advisory warning stickers. Frank Zappa, Twisted Sister and John Denver all campaigned against them.

? where did the band thin lizzie get their name

Thin Lizzie were named after *The Beano*'s Tin Lizzie. Original guitarist and comic fan Eric Bell suggested it, and Lynott's Dublin accent turned 'Tin' into 'Thin'.

? y r the band super furry animals in the guinness book of records

The Super Furry Animals are in the *Guinness Book of World Records* for the longest EP title – Llanfairpwllgwyngyllgogerychwyrn-drobwllllantysiliogogogoch (In Space)'.

? which group had their first 3 no. 1 hits in 1984

Frankie Goes to Hollywood are the band who had their first three No. 1 hits in 1984. They spent a total of 15 weeks at No. 1 in 1984.

? what was the only album to go to number 1 in 40 different countries

Madonna's album *Confessions on a Dance Floor* made No. 1 in 41 different countries, debuting at the top spot in 29 of them. It has sold 8 million copies.

? who has had the most hits but not a number 1 hit in the uk

Depeche Mode are the group with the most hits without ever having a No. 1. They have had 42 chart entries and never got a record beyond No. 4.

which drummer uses the largest drum kit in the world

Red Hot Chili Peppers drummer Chad Smith entered the *Guinness Book of World Records* for playing the world's largest drum kit, consisting of 308 pieces.

what's the longest song ever recorded

Chris Butler's 1996, 69-minute, 500-verse single 'The Devil's Glitch' is the longest recorded pop song. Butler wrote The Waitresses' 'Christmas Wrapping'.

what was the name of ian fleming's home

Ian Fleming lived in Jamaica in a property called Goldeneye. James Bond was named after an American ornithologist, author of *Birds of the West Indies*.

? lily allen, depeche mode and flaming lips have all recorded songs in which language

Lily Allen, Depeche Mode and Flaming Lips have all recorded songs in Simlish, the language spoken by the characters in the popular computer game *The Sims*.

? two word name type of theatrical spotlight also title of last uk number one single for successful pop group

Super Trouper is the name of a range of theatrical spotlights – and also the title of the last UK No. 1 single for the pop group ABBA in 1980.

? what period was the quill used for

The quill pen was the writing implement of choice from around AD 700 and was widely used until the steel dip pen took over in the late 18th century.

? musical instruments starting with c

Musical instruments starting with the letter C include clarinet, cello, contrabassoon, calliope, cymbals, cuica, Croix Sonore and the amplified cactus.

? are there any 20s, 30s or 40s songs that are about illness or feeling sick

In July 1941, George Formby released a song called 'Auntie Maggie's Remedy', the lyrics of which contained ailments including lumbago, rheumatics and gout.

? what does the saying 'arse and pockets' mean – or it cd be 'arse in pockets'

The saying 'arse and pockets' describes someone who is wearing badly fitting, too large clothes, and comes from James Joyce's *Ulysses*, published in 1922.

what was number 1 in the charts on 23.10.71

Rod Stewart's 'Maggie May' was the No. 1 single on 23 October 1971. Before his singing career, Stewart was an apprentice at Brentford Football Club.

who was on nevermind

Nirvana's 1991 album *Nevermind* features a 3-month-old infant named Spencer Elden swimming underwater and chasing a dollar bill on a hook. He is now 18.

what 60s song ends with the word nose

The 1965 track 'What's New Pussycat?' sung by Tom Jones ends with the word nose. The single was the theme title song to Clive Donner's film of the same name.

what new order song is on the trainspotting album

'Temptation' is the New Order song which appears on the *Trainspotting* soundtrack album (1996). In the film, Diane sings it in the bath.

who said you get them piping hot

The then-unknown Elvis Presley sang 'You can get 'em piping hot after 4pm' in a 1954 television commercial for Southern Made Doughnuts.

who wrote the children's song twinkle, twinkle little star

Jane Taylor was an English poet who wrote the words for the song 'Twinkle, Twinkle, Little Star' in 1806. It was originally entitled 'The Star'.

why did ravel the composer write a concerto for 1 hand

Ravel's 'Piano Concerto for the Left Hand' was composed in 1930 for his friend, Austrian composer Paul Wittgenstein, who lost his right arm in World War One.

who invented zero

It is believed that the Mayas created the number 0. The number 0 is the most significant contribution of non-western culture to mathematics.

? in the 12 days of xmas what does 3 french hens signify

In the festive song 'Twelve Days of Christmas', the three French hens signify theological virtues in the form of charity, faith and hope.

? what is the most remixed tune ever

The most remixed song ever is 'I Feel Loved' by Depeche Mode. There are 862 known remixes, but few are official releases. It was first released in 2001.

? where did the band nickelback get their name from

Nickelback's name originates from the nickel in change that band member Mike Kroeger often had to give customers in his previous job at Starbucks.

**? song manic street preachers
t m a t c**

> The Manic Street Preachers song
> beginning with the letters T M A T C
> is 'The Masses Against The Classes'. It
> was the first No. 1 of the 21st century.

**? what is the most played
song ever on world radio**

> The most played song ever on world
> radio is 'You've Lost That Lovin'
> Feelin'' by The Righteous Brothers:
> the equivalent of 45.6 continuous
> years' airplay.

**? who was the 1st person to
beatbox during a song**

> Doug E. Fresh was the first person to
> beatbox during a song, on the Top
> Flight Records single 'Pass the Boo-
> Dah'. The single was released in 1983.

**? why is the colour green
called green**

> The word 'green' derives from the Old
> English verb 'growan', which means
> 'to grow'. The wavelength of the
> colour is 520–570 nanometres.

? what is a word called when it spells something forwards and a different word backwards

A word that spells a different word backwards is a semordnilap (palindromes backwards). They are also known as volvograms. 'Stressed' is the longest.

? where does the saying 'the whole nine yards' come from

World War Two Spitfire planes' bullet belts were nine yards long. A pilot shooting all the bullets at the target would therefore give it 'the whole nine yards'.

? wot is the definition of anti-distablishmentarialism

Antidisestablishmentarianism opposes separation of church and state. The longest word in the dictionary is pneumonoultramicroscopicsilicovolcanoconiosis.

why is oddbins the off licence called this

In 1963, Ahmed Pochee started up a small business delivering bin-ends and oddments of wine to the restaurants and clubs of the West End – hence 'Oddbins'.

what english band had a no. 1 in new zealand and not in england

Joy Division got to No. 1 in New Zealand in 1981 with both 'Love Will Tear Us Apart' (a UK No. 13) and 'Atmosphere' (which didn't chart until 1988).

give me an ode or ditty to my geordie mate who hits 40 on friday

A rhyme for your mate's 40th: Another year, another wrinkle, pet. You don't half set the pace. We chipped in for the perfect gift – an iron for your face.

? **where did the term flip the bird come from, as in to stick one's middle finger up**

In 19th century English theatre, 'giving someone the bird' meant hissing them, like a goose, to convey disapproval. Hence 'flipping the bird'.

? **what is the quickest time anyone has ever spoken hamlet's to be or not to be speech**

Sean Shannon can recite Hamlet's 260-word 'To be or not to be' soliloquy in a record 23.8 seconds. It'd take him 45 minutes 5 seconds to recite all 29,551 words of the play.

? **what is the collective term for a group of idiots**

It's a thicket of idiots. It's also a stumble of drunks, baffle of noobs, horde of misers, lust of prostitutes and dork of Trekkies.

8

planes, trains and automobiles

From the tiny, cheap Tata Nano car to the Boeing 747 jumbo jet, motorised methods of transport are brilliant. If you disagree, try walking to Indonesia. Rather brilliantly, AQA 63336 knows how they work, when and why they don't work, how slow or fast they go and when they leave or arrive.

? what pop star has a fetish for model trains

The pop star who has a scale model of New York's Grand Central train station is Rod Stewart. He was spotted with a copy of *Model Railroader* in his car.

? what did mary ward do in offaly in ireland, in 1869

Mary Ward was the first fatal motor accident victim. The accident happened in Offaly in Ireland in 1869, on a drive around the Birr Castle estate.

? what causes 20 percent of car accidents in sweden

Almost 20% of Swedish car accidents are caused by elk. Swedish car makers Saab have a 'moose test' which involves crashing a car into a realistic model or swerving around it.

❓ what exploded in 1869 killing a policeman

The first ever set of traffic lights, outside the Houses of Parliament, exploded on 2 January 1869, killing the policeman who operated them.

❓ what do motorbikes nappies bibles written in zulu and cider brandy have in common

Motorbikes, nappies, Bibles written in Zulu, and cider brandy were all spilled by the cargo ship MSC *Napoli* when it ran aground off the coast of Branscombe in Devon.

❓ which bridge in london is insured as a ship

Tower Bridge is insured as a ship, by Lloyd's of London. It is the only movable bridge on the River Thames, and was originally staffed by ex-sailors.

? what are the strangest things that have been found on the tube

The following have all been found at Lost Property on London Underground: an urn containing ashes, breast implants, a coffin, and a 14-foot boat.

? can you tell me the best way to get to mexico if you are afraid of flying and you live in aylesbury

Leave Southampton on the *QE2* to New York, cruise to Los Angeles via Mexico, get the train to New York, then get the *QE2* home. Round trip of 29 days.

? what is the highest escalator in the world

The longest single-span escalator in the world (126m) is in Moscow, at the Park Pobedy metro station. The longest escalator system is in Hong Kong.

? if i was 2 park cars nose 2 tail how many would i need 2 fill up the channel tunnel

It would take 11,050 cars parked head to tail to fill the Channel Tunnel. There are 33 million cars in the UK – enough to fill 2,986 Channel Tunnels.

? why is the michelin tyre man white and plastic, when real tyres are black and rubber

Bibendum, the Michelin Man, is white because tyres were white or beige when he was introduced in 1898. Carbon black was added as a preservative in 1912.

? which is the steepest escalator on the london underground

The steepest escalators on the London Underground are at Angel station. They have a vertical rise of 27.4m (90ft) and a length of 60m (197ft).

what plane had the biggest propeller

The Soviet airlifter Antonov An-22 is the world's largest propeller plane. It has 4 x 5.6m Kuznetsov NK-12MA turboprops and is nicknamed 'Cock'.

who founded mclaren

McLaren, founded in 1963 by New Zealander Bruce McLaren (1937–70), is an F1 team based in Woking, UK. McLaren had one leg shorter than the other.

how much would it cost me per mile to fly to new zealand via la

It costs just 8p a mile to fly from Heathrow to Auckland via Los Angeles. This is less than half the cost of the fuel for driving a car in the UK today.

how much fuel does the queen elizabeth 2 use when crossing the atlantic

The *QE2* uses 171,805 tonnes of fuel to cross the Atlantic, compared to 228.2 million tonnes of oil used in the UK in the first quarter of 2008 alone.

what was the tube's first nickname

'The Tube' dates from 1900, when a line from Bank to Shepherd's Bush opened. Cylindrical tunnels and a 2d fare earned it the nickname 'twopenny tube'.

how many times did charles darwin sail to south america

Once. Charles Darwin spent five years on HMS *Beagle*, making a survey of South America between 1831 and 1836. On his return, aged 27, he never left England again.

how far can a 747 glide if all the engines cut out at full altitude (35k feet)

A 747 can glide 15km for every km it loses in height. 35,000ft is equivalent to 10.668km, so the stricken craft could glide for 160.02km.

what is the highest international airport in europe

The highest international airport in Europe is Poprad-Tatry Airport in Slovakia, at 2,356 feet (718m) elevation. It services a nearby ski resort town.

if santa were real, how long would it take him to deliver presents to everyone's house

If Santa travelled at 75 mph to deliver presents, it would take him 55,555 days (152 years) to cover the whole world. Luckily he can go faster.

? what is the more carbon-efficient method of transport, plane or ship, and does this change with distance

Ships are more carbon-efficient per kilo of freight than planes, over any distance, but account for 5% of global emissions compared with 2% for planes.

? in which year did the paris metro underground start

The Paris Metro opened on 19 July 1900. It has the most closely spaced underground stations in the world, with 245 of them within 16 square miles.

? what speed was the first speeding ticket issued for

The first speeding ticket was issued to Mr Walter Arnold in 1896. He was fined 1 shilling for doing 8 mph in a 2 mph zone. The first road death was also recorded in 1896.

? what is the fastest road car in the world

The SSC Ultimate Aero TT holds the speed record for a production car, at 256.1 mph. The Bugatti Veyron is second, with a top speed of 253.2 mph.

? what is the smallest car

The world's smallest car is a 1960s P50 Microcar, which is 1.34m long, 99cm wide and 1.34m tall. The Smart car is the smallest current car, at 2.5m long.

? what is the biggest car

The longest car in the world is a limousine 30.5m long, owned by Jay Ohrberg of California. It has a pool with a diving board and is used in movies.

? what car was launched at 1948 motor show and sold 1.6 million

The 1948 Motor Show at Earls Court saw the launch of the Morris Minor. 1.6 million were produced at the plant at Cowley, Oxfordshire, up to 1971.

？ which country has the highest car crash rate in europe

> Greece has the highest car accident rate in Europe. The Republic of Ireland has Europe's highest rate of fatalities caused by car accidents.

？ does having your air conditioning on in the car use extra petrol or is it just a myth

> It is partly true: at less than 50 mph it is more fuel efficient to leave your windows down, but over 50 mph, air conditioning is more fuel efficient.

？ what colour was the first saab and why

> The first Saab (Model 92) was green. The colour was 'chosen' as Saab had an excess of this colour of paint after the end of wartime aircraft production.

why do harley-davidsons sound like they do

Harley-Davidsons are V-twin engines with the pistons mounted at 45 degrees. This causes them to fire at uneven intervals, giving the distinctive sound.

what is a tata nano

The Tata Nano is an Indian car made by Tata Motors. It will be the world's cheapest car. It is due to go on sale later in 2008 for 100,000 rupees, or £1,277.

how many cars are on the road in the uk

There are 33 million vehicles on UK roads, including cars, vans, taxis, buses and lorries. 26 million of them are cars. 2.5 million are company cars.

? what is the fastest speed anyone has gone on a motorcycle

The fastest speed anyone has ever attained on a motorcycle is 350.8 mph. This was achieved by Chris Carr on the Bonneville Salt Flats, Utah, on 5 September 2006.

? what came first, the polo car or the polo mint

The Polo mint came first, in 1948. The VW Polo hit the roads in 1975. Polo, the sport, was first played in 700 BC by the Persians, in epic 100-a-side matches.

? car built before 1919 called what

Any car built before 1919 was called 'veteran'. Cars built between January 1919 and December 1930 were called 'vintage'. Cars built after 1930 were 'classic'.

how many aeroplanes are in the world

There are 260,000 serviceable aeroplanes in the world. 200,000 of these are commercial aeroplanes. 3,500 are in the air at any one time.

has anyone ever cheated (and then been disqualified) at the tour de france by taking the train

In 1904, Maurice Garin was disqualified from the Tour de France for taking the train. He had won the year before, without the need for public transport.

has higher petrol meant less traffic

Yes. As a result of soaring fuel prices, car traffic on UK roads fell by 2% during the second quarter of 2008 compared with the same period in 2007.

planet earth

From the moment that it emerged from the Big Bang, Planet Earth has been an enormous oblate spheroid of brilliance. Wherever you are on Earth, AQA 63336 has all the answers, like these corkers about the planet itself and its brilliant inhabitants.

what is the hottest recorded temperature on earth

The hottest ever recorded temperature of 57.7°C occurred 22 years before the invention of suntan lotion in Al 'Aziziyah, Libya, on 13 September 1922.

has any animal got 2 hearts

There is no animal with just two hearts. Squid, oysters and octopuses have three hearts. Hagfish have five. Earthworms have multiple hearts, but only Doctor Who has two.

when was the first map created

The oldest map dates back to about 10,000 BC and was discovered in Ukraine in 1966. It is inscribed on a mammoth tusk and shows dwellings along a river.

any hells on earth

Hell is a village in Stjordal, Norway, with a population of 352. It regularly freezes over. There are also Hells in Michigan, California and Grand Cayman.

what do you think would happen if the oceans turned to beer

If the oceans turned to beer it would indicate Jesus was up to his old tricks. Increasing numbers of dolphins would be done for drunk diving.

what is the foggiest city in australia

Canberra, the capital, is the foggiest city in Australia. It has 46 foggy days a year, 28 of them in May–August. Brisbane has 20 foggy days and Darwin only two.

what's the world record for the quickest time taken to pop 100 balloons

A dog called Anastasia set the Guinness World Record for the quickest time taken to pop 100 balloons. She popped the lot with her mouth in 44.8 seconds.

how many true and false ribs do horses have

The horse has eight sets of true ribs and ten sets of false ribs, making 36 ribs altogether. Some breeds, e.g. the Arab, have one less vertebra and only 34 ribs.

what % of the uk is afraid of spiders

Fear of spiders (arachnophobia) is the most common phobia: it affects 62% of the population. Over 65s and East Anglians are the least scared.

why do male dogs lick the floor where another dog has had a wee

The dog is 'checking out' the other dog by sniffing its urine. The jaw movement is called the flehmen gesture, and helps him analyse the pheromones.

what is fordlandia

Fordlandia is the name of a piece of land in Brazil that was purchased in the 1920s by Henry Ford, founder of the car firm. His aim was to source rubber.

what is the highest pub in europe

The Frog and Roastbeef in Val Thorens in France is the highest pub in Europe. It is located in the French Alps at an altitude of 2,300 metres.

what noise does a pig make in french as in english it says oink

In French, pigs go 'groin groin'. In German they go 'grunz', and in Japanese they go 'boo boo'. Pigs do not actually sweat, despite the common saying.

how do dog whelks breathe

Like most marine gastropods, dog whelks respire using a gill-like structure, the ctenidium. Land snails have a lung, taking in air through a pneumostome.

? how many times does a bat's heart beat in a minute

The heart of a medium-sized bat beats at a rate of 700 times per minute, 1,000 while flying, and a mere 25 while waiting out the winter season.

? in what way are the tides in the solent unusual

The Solent has two extra high tides each day, or 'Double High Water'. A circular current travels around the Isle of Wight and back through the Solent again.

? how can i stop myself from turning into an antelope

To stop yourself from turning into an antelope, try to concentrate on un-antelopish thoughts, such as the stock market, Marmite sandwiches or surfing.

? which animal has sex the longest

Insects are the creatures that have sex for the longest time – up to 60 hours. Their genitals often lock together. Snakes can have sex for 24 hours.

how many ants could you fit in a jumbo jet and it can still take off

The average ant weighs 3mg. A jumbo jet containing 46,500,000,000 of them would still be able to take off (assuming one of them knew how to fly a plane).

on average how many new species are found each day in borneo

On average, a new species is found in Borneo every nine days. In 2006, scientists found a new species every week – including a tree frog with green eyes.

what is the biggest edible fungus in the world

The world's biggest edible fungus is a Honey Mushroom colony in Oregon, USA. It is 3.5 miles wide and covers the equivalent of 1,665 football pitches.

? is beer bad for cats

Beer is indeed bad for cats. Alcohol is highly toxic to felines: e.g. two teaspoonfuls of whisky could put a cat into a coma, and a tablespoonful could kill it.

? how long would it take a person to drink the sea

It would take a person 143,737,166,324 million years to drink the 1,260 million trillion litres of water on earth, at a rate of 1l/hr with no loo breaks.

? what is the name for a column of ice amongst crevasses on a glacier

A serac is a pinnacle or tower of ice in a crevasse. It's also a type of cheese (similar to ricotta) made from whey in the Savoie region in France.

? what were jellyfish called before jelly was invented

Jellyfish were called medusas until 1841, but the word 'jelly' dates back to 1381. Of culinary importance in China, they're eaten as 'water-mothers'.

? where did all the water on our planet come from

Icy comets and asteroids were the source of present-day water on earth. When they passed into the warm atmosphere, the ice was released as water vapour.

? why do we and other animals cock our heads when we don't understand or are confused

Humans and animals cock their heads when confused to allow better identification of sounds and images by listening and looking in a different plane.

? is there still a bounty on squirrels

No. The Forestry Committee introduced a bounty of 6d (2.5p) a tail for grey squirrels in 1932, but stopped it in 1957. In 1999, £1 a tail was briefly offered.

? can butterflies break trees

Monarch butterflies over-winter in the mountains west of Mexico City. Tens of millions of butterflies settle, often breaking branches with their weight.

? how do you treat a fish with an air bubble: our fish keeps floating to the top of the tank and struggles to swim down

To treat air bubbles in fish, isolate the fish and feed it only tiny pieces of squashed peas to help pass the air. When it recovers, return to the tank.

what are the little 5

The 'Little 5' African animals are buffalo weaver, elephant shrew, leopard tortoise, ant lion and rhino beetle. They share parts of their name with the 'Big 5'.

how many rabbits were on the ark after 40 days

After 40 days, there would have been a maximum total of fourteen rabbits on the Ark. A rabbit's gestation period is 29–35 days and they can have a litter of twelve.

how long is a horse gut

A horse's gut (small and large intestines) is approximately 26m long and holds up to 40 gallons of matter. The food must travel around 180 bends.

what are woody pigs

'Woody pigs' is slang for woodlice, as is 'doodlebug', 'roly-poly', 'chiggy pig', 'cheeselog', 'gramfer', 'pill bug', 'roll up bug' and 'slater'. The UK has 37 species.

do frogs or toads close their eyes every time they eat

All frogs and toads blink when they swallow. No bone exists between the eye and mouth, so the eye is pushed against the roof of the mouth, forcing food down.

how many sharks are killed every year

Compared to the 10–15 humans killed by sharks each year, humans kill over 100 million sharks annually, and some species are now very close to extinction.

is cheeta still alive

Tarzan chimpanzee Cheeta (aka Jiggs) is alive, aged 76. He plays the piano and paints. His ghost-written autobiography, *Me Cheeta*, is due to be published in October 2008.

is there a place called nipple

Nipple is a place in Utah, USA. Molly's Nipple is also in Utah. Susie's Nipple and Squaw Tit are in Idaho, USA. Nipple Peak is in Antarctica.

? why is it that a fly will always move out of the way when i try and swat it even tho my reactions are pretty much as quick as bruce lee

Flies can't predict the future. They have a fast escape reflex, making them jump away from swats coming towards them. They can react in 1/50 of a second.

? what is the mull of kintyre's link to porn

The angle of the Mull of Kintyre was unofficially used by the British Board of Film Classification as a limit to the erect state of a penis on film.

? which is cleverer: a dog or a budgie

Dogs are cleverer than budgies. Labrador Endal put his owner into recovery position, covered him with a blanket and summoned help. A budgie would only squawk.

how long is an ant-eater's tongue

A giant ant-eater's tongue is 60cm long and can be flicked in and out of the mouth 150 times per minute. From nose to tail, the giant ant-eater is 1.8m long.

what is the name of the animal in capetown that looks like a rabbit but comes from the elephant family

The dassie or hyrax (Procavia capensis) resembles an oversized guinea pig, but is actually closely related to elephants, manatees and dugongs.

what is 70cm in inches

70cm is 27.56 inches, 2.3 feet or 0.76 yards. This is the world record for a pig's jump, achieved by Kotetsu, a pot-bellied pig, on 22 August 2004.

? what type of frog ribbets

The Pacific tree frog (Pseudacris regilla) is the only frog to make the 'ribbit' sound. It is the state frog of Washington and is able to change colour.

? did a polar bear from london zoo ever catch its dinner in the thames

In the 13th century, a polar bear was kept as part of the Tower of London menagerie, and fished in the Thames for salmon whilst attached to a leash.

? do all cows point north

On average, cows face five degrees off the geographic north or south poles. Observations of deer herds and their snow tracks reveal a similar trend.

? if an ant was the same size as a human, how fast would it be able to run

If an ant was the same size as a human, it would travel twice as fast as a Lamborghini. An ant-sized human would travel at a measly 0.5cm per second.

? when did london become capital and what was the capital before

London replaced Winchester as England's capital after the Norman Conquest, which began in 1066. Perth was Scotland's capital before Edinburgh.

sex, philosophy and life

Without sex, there would be no life. Philosophy is an attempt to make sense of both. Casanova was brilliant at sex, while Socrates was brilliant at philosophy. Meanwhile, AQA 63336 encourages everyone to be brilliant at life; and the following chapter shows how.

which is the only country in europe where you can marry someone who's already dead

According to French law, a marriage between a living person and a dead person can take place as long as it can be shown they had intended to marry.

i'm in love with a sheep: how do i get it to love me back

Sadly, there is no way of getting the sheep to love you. It is a selfish animal that largely thinks about grass. Console yourself with a woolly jumper.

tell me a hebrew chat-up line

Hebrew chat-up lines: *At yafa ahuvati* ('You're beautiful, my love'), *ani meta alecha* ('I'm crazy for you'), *hatakhtonim sheli akhilim* ('my underwear's edible').

? what do you buy a man who has everything

You can buy the man who has everything something they already have but will shortly expire – e.g. goat's cheese, teenage girlfriends, computer accessories.

? what gives

Santa Claus gives many gifts at Christmas. He is based on St Nicholas, patron saint of sailors, who was just 5ft tall and had a broken nose.

? which landmark would brits most like to have sex at

Wembley Stadium topped the list of landmarks where Brits would most like to have sex. It was followed by Stonehenge in second place and the London Eye in third.

? are turtles passionate when they hump

Turtles can sound passionate; the male will often roar, groan, hiss and make other comical noises. Box turtles may bite. Mating can last several hours.

? i fancy the doll ken, should i kill barbie to help me get with him

If you killed Barbie, Ken would never forgive you. Ken has a wonderful best friend called Allan ('born' in 1963). Set your sights on him instead.

? is nothing something

Nothing is something. It is a concept that can be expressed and understood, even though it does not exist. It's also the reciprocal of infinity.

? when's the latest you can have kids

Unless affected by health problems, men produce sperm all their lives, although it gets less likely to fertilise. Pablo Picasso fathered a child at 90.

? **is it ok to be sexually attracted to dogs**

It is normal to be sexually attracted to dogs, but only if you are a dog yourself – in which case AQA is impressed by your ability to send texts.

? **which area in england has the highest women to men ratio**

The London borough of Kensington and Chelsea has the highest ratio of single women to single men. It is also one of the wealthiest areas in the UK.

? **does sex pre-match hinder your performance on the pitch**

Recent studies show that this is not the case, as sex has no effect on strength or focus. It may in fact help improve co-ordination.

? has there ever been an erection on british television

An erect penis was shown on British TV in 1991 when the *The TV They Tried To Ban* documentary showed a scene from Derek Jarman's *Sebastiane* (1976).

? wot does 'iyot' mean, it may be a thai word

Iyot is the Filipino word for sex. *Nagiyot* means 'had sex', *gaiyot* means 'currently having sex', and, bizarrely, *mangingiyot* means 'photographer'.

? what are snail's love darts and what are they for

When two snails meet, mating is initiated by one piercing the skin of the other with a calcified 'love dart'. It is thought to stimulate sperm exchange.

? is lion sex painful if so why

Yes. The male lion's penis has spines which point backwards. Upon withdrawal of the penis, the spines rake the walls of the female's vagina.

? am i alive

AQA believes that if you possess the ability to send a text message, then you are indeed alive. You text, therefore you are.

? what is the difference between things

The difference between things is what remains when one is subtracted from the other. For example, the difference between a lollipop and a sweet is a stick.

? write me a special poem about judith

Oh Judith, can I call you Judy? I look at you and I feel broody. Your name's impossible to rhyme with, it's you I want to spend my time with.

? a romantic way of telling someone we are going hot air ballooning

Tell them that together there is nothing that you cannot do, even touch the sky. Or say that you want to soar like your heart does when you see them.

? what is the world's longest engagement

The world's longest engagement lasted 67 years. Octavio Guillen and Adriana Martinez were 15 when they got engaged, and 82 on their wedding day.

? has there ever been a couple married in an asda store in the uk

Jill and Pete Freeman were married in the clothing section of their local Asda in York in February 2004. They left to a bagpipe version of the Asda tune.

how many couples in uk

There are 11,926,564 married couples, 3,500 gay civil unions and 2.2 million unmarried couples in the UK, making a total of 14,130,064 couples.

do people who are assholes actually know they are assholes

Everyone thinks that they are normal and well liked, even the assholes. However, someone who is an asshole to you will be another person's best friend.

how do you get monster calves like the girl in front

You could get monster calves by eating an excess of protein and rigorous weight training (unless you mean cattle, in which case inbreeding is recommended).

what shall i get sarah for christmas: she's my 22 year old girlfriend, she likes the internet, surreal things and shoes

You should get Sarah a new mouse, *The Smell of Reeves & Mortimer* on DVD and a pair of Jimmy Choos. Salvador Dali wi-fi sandals are not yet available.

whats the 3 things you should not talk about when you are in the pub

When in a pub never talk about Paris Hilton, as she's irrelevant; nor the recession, as no one wants to be reminded; nor your boss, as he's behind you.

what can i do to make lizz forgive me: i need a really original and cute gesture

Stand under her window and release balloons with 'Sorry' written on them. Tell her 'I'm sorry to high heaven' as they float upward. Be sure you mean it.

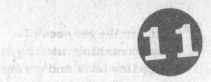

the most bizarre

AQA 63336 researchers aren't easily fazed. To answer some of the odder questions requires a broad mind, a strong stomach and a monitor that can't be seen by any children. Others merely require the ability to raise an eyebrow. We're happy to answer anything, but sometimes even we wonder why anyone would ask such things.

? **what are the chances of a meteor crashing into the back of my head and giving me superhuman powers**

There's a 1 in 196 trillion chance of a meteor crashing into your head and giving you superhuman powers. That's like winning the Lotto jackpot twice in a row.

? **if you came out of your home and turned left 3 times and arrived back home to meet a man in a mask, who is the masked man**

The masked man is the catcher in a game of baseball. You have just scored a home run by running around three bases and returning to home base.

? how many words do you need to have invented to have created your own language

To create a language, you need 10,000 words or more. Volapuk was created in 1879–80 by Johann Martine Schleyer. Esperanto was created seven years later.

? if music is the food of love why can't rabbits sing

Music is truly the food of love. Rabbits can't sing because they don't feel love, only lust. Romantic love, like music, is a fundamentally human concept.

? can you legally bury someone in your own back garden

Under the Burial Laws Amendment 1880, you can legally bury someone in your back garden, though a body is defined as 'clinical waste' and mustn't pollute.

? when i listen to radio and
the song reach for the stars
comes on by s club 7 i sit
and bounce on a football:
will it do me harm

> Occasionally bouncing on a football
> will not do you any harm.
> Overexposure to S Club 7 can lead to
> serious consequences, like the loss of
> all self-worth.

? i was born in outer space,
what nationality am i

> The Outer Space Treaty of 1967
> (ratified by 98 states) follows the
> tradition of maritime law – you have
> the nationality of the spaceship you
> were born in.

? how many trees does it take
to make 17.3 billion
matchsticks

> One tree makes 1m matchsticks, so
> 17,300 trees make 17.3bn
> matchsticks. There are 600bn trees in
> the world – enough for 600
> quadrillion matches.

? what's the worst bizarre experiment ever

Stubbins Ffirth tried to prove yellow fever wasn't contagious by pouring infected vomit into his eyes, inhaling it, frying it and drinking it. He was wrong.

? what is the fastest time anyone has completed the 100 metres on a space hopper

Ashrita Furman took 30.2 seconds to complete 100m on a spacehopper, and 15 minutes 3 seconds for one mile. He also holds the record for crushing 39 eggs with his head in 30 seconds.

? who was harry meadows

In 1961, the 87-year-old Harry Meadows accidentally killed three of his fellow care home residents by dressing as the Grim Reaper and peering in at the window.

? what 5 words would i say if i was standing on the edge of a high cliff, wearing only yellow furry slippers

> Standing on the edge of a cliff in yellow furry slippers, you'd say: 'I want better Christmas presents.' People will understand your plight.

? what strange piece of lost property was left at hanoi airport

> A Boeing 727 was left at Hanoi's Noi Bai Airport. It was flown in from Siem Reap, Cambodia, in late 2007 and remains unclaimed. Its logo says 'Air Dream'.

? why should i be scared on friday april 13th 2029

> An asteroid called 2004 MN4 will come scarily close to Earth on Friday 13 April 2029. It'll be within 19,000 miles of Earth, but it won't hit.

? hi aqa how do u do, i have a question 4u: can u tell me a fact about middlewich town – please do not frown, but to keep the rhythm flowin, can u reply as a poem

> AQA would never frown, as Middlewich is a market town, set in Cheshire county. Once famed for cheese, farms and silk gowns, the parish was quite a bounty.

? when did people start having conversations x

> Human speech developed 200,000 years ago. Conversation started five minutes after that, when it was discovered that talking to yourself made you look weird.

? how many people per year drop their ipods down the toilet

> 11,000 iPods a year end up in the toilet – 31 per day. Apple has sold 130 million iPods worldwide. Let it dry out fully before re-using it.

? when would a snail from bristol who wanted to go to the olympic games in london have to leave to get there in time

It should have left two years ago to travel the 118 miles from Bristol to London in 2,198 days, at 1mm per second. King's Lynn hosts the snail racing championship.

? has anyone ever got their name from a phone book

When C. Kalms and M. Mindel opened their first shop in Southend in 1937, they only had room for six letters on the shopfront and chose 'Dixons' from the phone book.

? what's the most unhappy onion

The unhappiest onion is pickled – always sour and vinegary. The happiest onion is a spring onion – always bouncy. Yellow onions are the most cowardly.

name five pop groups whose name includes part of somebody's house

Basement Jaxx, The Doors, Lord Kitchener, The Spiral Starecase, The Yardbirds, and Loo and Placido are pop groups with parts of a house in their names.

is winston churchill a dog

17% of school children aged 8–11 think Sir Winston Churchill is the talking bulldog in the Churchill insurance adverts. Just 52% know he was prime minister during World War Two.

who was the guy who used to eat planes and other objects

Monsieur Mangetout ('Mr Eat-All'; real name Michel Lotito) is the French entertainer who eats the indigestible. It took him two years to eat a Cessna 150.

? how much does it cost, assuming you can find them, to hire the a-team

It would cost £100m to hire the A-Team. This is due to inflation, and the cost of creating a lifelike robot of George Peppard (Hannibal), who died in 1994.

? how does chris walken get such lift in his hair

Christopher Walken pulls hard on his hair every day when watching the news, hence the lift. He read that President Kennedy used to do it to prevent baldness.

? police in northern india are paid an extra 30 rupees a month to wear what

Police in northern India are being paid an extra 30 rupees (37p) a month to grow moustaches to give them more authority. The world's longest was 3.81m.

? **is it true that road foundations are made from old books**

The M6 toll road in Birmingham was lined with 2.5 million pulped Mills & Boon novels when constructed in 2003. The paper pulp is a good sound absorber.

? **how many 5-year-olds could an average adult male human take in a fight**

A quintet of 5-year-olds could take down an adult male in a fight. Two ninja children would have the grown-up crying for his mummy and sucking his thumb.

? **i'm going to buy a crocodile and a frog, and mate them to create the ultimate dinosaur**

The frogodile is a vicious creature indeed. AQA suggests a large pen to keep it in, as it has been known to jump 10ft in the air to catch passing cuckhens.

? **if all the fruit in the world had a massive free for all (fight), who would emerge victorious**

> In a free for all fruit fight, the lethal coconut would win. It kills 150 people a year just by falling out of trees; just imagine if it got really mad.

? **how does one throw the holy handgrenade**

> To throw the Holy Hand Grenade: thou pullest the holy pin, then on the count of three, lobbest thou it in the direction of thine foe, who shall snuff it.

? **what year was it 1 billion minutes ago**

> A billion minutes ago, in AD 106, the Roman Empire was in full swing. A billion hours ago it was the Middle Paleolithic era. A billion seconds is 32 years.

? **if a man stands alone in a field speaking, and if there is no woman around him to hear, is he still wrong**

> Any man standing in a field talking to himself is a few sandwiches short of a picnic, so is wrong whatever he says. Pity his long-suffering wife.

? **who would win in a fight between a weeble, ewok, an oompa loompa and a ribenaberry**

> An Ewok will always win a fight. Weebles can only dodge a hit, Oompa-Loompas would break into song every five minutes and Ribenaberries would be easily squashed.

? **how many tyres would u need 2 stack on top of each other 2 reach the moon**

> The distance to the moon varies between 356,410km and 406,740km, while tyres stack at five to a metre. You will need 1.782–2.034 billion tyres, and long arms.

? how many cheese slices would it take to fill a ford ka

It would take 113,000 packaged cheese slices to completely fill the interior of a Ford Ka. That much cheese would cost you £8,362 from Sainsbury's.

? if there was a stannah stairlift built for my grandma from here to the moon how long would it take to get there

At 18ft per minute, a stairlift would take 133 years to travel the 238,896 miles to the moon. Thora Hird (who adverstised for rivals Churchill) lived to 91.

? what would you do if you
were scratching your ear
and a large antelope came
charging out of it followed
by a small mexican man
named jose shouting come
back here you promised me
a trip to the nunnery later

> The natural reaction would be to rope
> the ear-dwelling antelope, then use it
> to catch Jose. It would then be a case
> of forcing them back into your ear.

? what's the best place i can
go to (preferably a sunny
country) where the uk
government cannot
extradite me from

> Venezuela has great weather and no
> extradition treaty. When you want a
> break from crime, admire Angel Falls,
> the world's highest waterfall at 979m.

who would win in a fight between graham norton and a koala

The koala would defeat Graham Norton after a tense battle. Norton would start off cocky, but the koala would play cute before gouging his eyes out.

how many sheets of a4 paper would it take to cover reio diganero

It would take 2,015,451,800 sheets of A4 paper to cover Rio de Janeiro, which has an area of 1,260 sq km. A4 paper has an area of 626.67 sq cm.

how many fray bentos pies can you fit in a toilet

38 Fray Bentos pies fit in a toilet. They're named after a town in Uruguay where the Liebeg Extract of Meat Company had a factory. It's now a museum.

everything else

Some information refuses to fit neatly into any category, which is why most filing systems are dominated by a bulging folder marked 'miscellaneous' or 'gubbins', depending on the mood of the filing clerks. In this chapter, we gather together some of the brilliant answers from the AQA 63336 misc/gubbins folder.

? what, measuring 18 by 15 feet, did 146 enter and only 23 leave alive

The Black Hole of Calcutta was a dungeon in which 146 British troops were held overnight following the fall of Fort William on 20 June 1756. Just 23 survived.

? where is the longest bench in the world

The longest bench, at 460.9m, is on the Masuhogaura coast of Japan. It's made of wood, and offers romantic sunset views for you and 1,349 other people.

? is it true that city centre cctv cameras can talk to passers by

Talking CCTV cameras are not a wind-up. Seven of the cameras in Middlesbrough town centre allow operators to shout orders at those behaving antisocially.

how much waste is produced when making a phone

The amount of waste made when producing a mobile phone is 75kg. This is called the ecological rucksack. A toothbrush's is 1.5kg, a computer's 1,500kg.

what were the crosshairs on telescopes made from in the past

Threads taken from the cocoon of the brown recluse spider were used to make crosshairs. The very fine, strong spider silk made excellent crosshair.

why is apple computers called apple

The founders of Apple Computers chose the name so that it would come before rivals Atari in the telephone directory.

? please name lots of things that are known by a brand name such as hoover

Other products known by a brand name: Sellotape, Blu-Tack, Xerox, Thermos, Kleenex, Biro, Filofax, Durex, Play-Doh, Aspirin, Escalator, Jacuzzi, Walkman.

? what sort of things weigh 50 tons

50 tons is around the same as 9.3 African elephants, 3.6 Big Bens, 68 cows, 51 shire horses, 280 female lions or 2,800 microwave ovens.

? what else did the creator of wonder woman invent

William Moulton Marston, the creator of Wonder Woman, invented the systolic blood-pressure test in the 1920s, as used in a polygraph (lie detector).

? who invented the game tetris, when, and when did it go electronic

Tetris was invented by a Soviet mathematician called Alexey Pajitnov in 1985 on an Electronika 60 – a computer with just 250khz processing speed.

? what was invented in c16th, banned in c19th, and reinstated in c20th

Queen Elizabeth I held the first national lottery in 1567. Lotteries were banned in 1826, and returned in 1994. A lottery paid for Westminster Bridge in 1730.

? if a lemon can power a lightbulb can enough lemons power a television

A lemon produces 0.0007 watts of power. A TV uses about 80–200 watts when on and 0.8–1.1 watts on standby. So 200,000 lemons are needed (1,400 on standby).

❓ is the queen's residence in sandringham on gmt or does it have its own time zone

Until 1936, all 180 clocks in the Royal clock collection at Sandringham were set on 'Sandringham time', half an hour ahead of GMT.

❓ where is the smallest house in the uk

The smallest house in the UK is a 6-foot-wide house in Conwy, at the Quay, in north Wales. A 7-foot man once lived there – on his own.

❓ criptic for flower of london six letters

The answer for the cryptic clue 'Flower of London' would be Thames, a 'flow-er' of London. The Thames runs for 215 miles, all within England.

**my 8 year old son finn
wants to know if magnets
ever lose their magnetism**

> Magnets lose a very small fraction of
> their magnetism over time, but only
> 1% of their power over ten years.
> Heat and other magnets affect their
> power.

**what is the biggest
snowball ever made**

> The world's largest snowball was 21ft
> 3in in circumference and 2.06m in
> diameter. It was rolled by US students
> on 10 February 2006.

**what was the first ever
published comic strip**

> The first published comic strip was
> Richard Outcault's 'Yellow Kid', which
> first appeared in the *New York
> Journal* on 24 October 1897.

? which indian tribe sold the island of manhattan (nyc)

The Canarsee tribe sold Manhattan Island to Peter Minuit of the Dutch West India Company on 4 May 1626. He paid 60 guilders (about $24) for it.

? why isn't the rotherhithe tunnel straight

The Rotherhithe Tunnel was built with bends so that horses would not be able to see the light at the other end and bolt for the exit.

? are there still unexploded bombs in the river thames from world war 2

London has an estimated 5,057 unexploded bombs from World War Two. Many of these were dropped in the Docklands area and can still be found in the Thames.

why is the new forest called the new forest

In 1079, William the Conqueror claimed the New Forest as a royal hunting preserve, naming it 'Nova' ('new'), as it was his first enclosed hunting ground.

what is the biggest painting in the world

The world's largest painting is David Aberg's 8,000 sq m *Mother Earth*. It took 2.5 years and 100 tons of paint to produce it in a Swedish aircraft hangar.

what is a mountain in scotland below 3000 and above 2500ft

Corbetts are peaks in Scotland between 2,500 and 3,000ft, named in the 1920s after John Rooke Corbett. Grahams are hills between 2,000 and 2,499ft.

? which is the smallest of america's great lakes

Lake Ontario is the smallest of the Great Lakes in terms of surface area, but the second smallest in volume. Lake Erie is the smallest lake by volume.

? when was the first uk patent

The first UK patent was granted by King Henry VI in 1449 to a Flemish man. It gave him a 20-year monopoly on the production of stained glass.

? what does the wd in wd40 stand for

WD-40 stands for 'Water Displacement, 40th formula'. It was developed in 1953 by Norm Larsen and first used to protect missiles from corrosion and rust.

where did the terms yahoo and blue tooth come from

The name Yahoo comes from the yobs of the same name in *Gulliver's Travels* by Jonathan Swift. Bluetooth was named after a late 10th-century king, Harald Bluetooth.

why are smiley faces yellow

The smiley face, first used by Harvey Ball, is yellow because the logo was influenced by Kolobok, a yellow spherical being in an East Slavic fairy tale.

i am 9 letters long, u can take a certain letter away from me, 1 at a time, and each time i still make a word right down to the last letter

A nine-letter word which makes a new word each time you deduct a letter is 'wrappings': 'wrapping', 'rapping', 'raping', 'aping', 'ping', 'pig', 'pi', 'i'.

? **do fish ever get thirsty i'm not a moron i'm just asking**

Fish don't get thirsty but do absorb water through their skin, by osmosis. Fish don't have a bladder. Their urine is excreted with their poo.

? **what are you wearing**

AQA is wearing a Great Britain Olympic vest, polka-dot socks and a pair of red underpants with the words 'love machine' embossed in gold.

? **if your given the freedom of the city what does that entail**

The freedom of the city originally allowed martial organisations to march with drums beating, colours flying and bayonets fixed. It now has no privileges.

? how many miles in a kilometre

> 1km is 0.62 miles. 1km is also equal to 2.25 Empire State Buildings, 168 small intestines, 82 T Rexes, 9,821 human tongues or 561 giraffe necks.

? what happened to the englishman the irishman and the welshman

> The Englishman, Irishman and Welshman have been suspended from the comedy lexicon, pending allegations of racial stereotyping and discrimination.

? what wud a perfect purse contain 4 a chief bridesmaid

> A chief bridesmaid should carry: tissues for wedding tears, lipstick for her and the bride, a small perfume spray, and a bar of chocolate for emergencies.

? are there more ear wigglers or italian speakers in the world

Ear wigglers. Italian is the first language of 63 million people, while 20% of the world's population can ear wiggle (1.32 billion people).

? weirdest named dinosaur

The dinosaur species Masiakasaurus knopfleri was named after Mark Knopfler. The paleontologists were listening to Dire Straits when they discovered it.

? what are the 2 most expensive spices in the world

Saffron is the most expensive spice in the world. It takes up to 250,000 saffron crocus flowers to make 1lb of spice. Pure vanilla is second most expensive.

? in what year was there either a strike in toilet roll industry or a shortage

There was a toilet roll shortage in the USA in 1973 after Johnny Carson announced, in jest, that there was a shortage. People panic-bought the next day.

? when did girls first start wearing jeans

Women started to wear jeans during the Second World War. They were worn by workers in munitions factories, where dresses and skirts were unsafe.

? when was the death penalty abolished in ireland

The death penalty was abolished in Ireland in 1990. The first European country to abolish it was Portugal, in 1867. The UK entirely abolished it in 1998.

? how many fighting countries constitute a world war

A world war is a military conflict spanning more than two continents, in which at least twenty major countries participate in an attack against a common enemy.

? which letter is most common at the beginning of capital cities

27 of the world's capital cities begin with the letter B. This is closely followed by the letter S, which has 26 capital cities beginning with it.

? a bus carrying 7 girls with 7 bags each with 7 cats each with 7 kittens, how many legs are there on the bus

A bus doesn't have legs. Nice try, though. The total number of legs on board the bus is 10,992: 1 bus driver (2); 7 girls (14); 343 cats (1,372); and 2,401 kittens (9,604).

who was the first major criminal to be arrested with the use of radio

Dr Crippen was the first murderer to be arrested by wireless. He was fleeing to Canada on board a ship in 1910 when the radio message came through.

how many roads are there in the city of london

There are no roads in the City of London. There are streets, and there are lanes and alleys, yards, gates and courts, but there is not a single road.

what was the first beer canned in the uk

The Felinfoel Brewery Company of Llanelli was the first to can beer in the UK, in December 1935. US companies had been producing canned beer since 1933.

? **is julie the most sincere honest person i know**

> Yes, Julie is a martyr to the truth, utterly honest and sincere. If Julie was going commando, and you asked her about her knickers, she'd reveal all.

? **how much does it cost to text u these questions: riddle it to me in your best joker answer**

> When there's an answer that cannot be found, text AQA – it costs only a pound. It'll send you the answer ASAP; you'll be glad you spent 100p.

the ones that didn't make it

Coming up with brilliant answers, time after time, isn't an easy job; which is why we only let the crème de la crème loose on your questions. When people apply, all we ask them to do is answer twelve questions, simple as that. But only one in twenty get through the selection process. Here are some of the answers from applicants that, needless to say, didn't make the grade. If you reckon you can do better, apply at www.aqa.63336.com.

? have we had a non c of e prime minister

AQA believes Gordon Brown is not a nonce. He is the sixth postwar PM to have not won an election, only has one eye and he will shortly lower interest rates.

? how many points will I get on my licence for going through a red light

Unfortunately dear, you will not get a point driving through the red light because it is against the driving rules.

? how can you tell if someone loves you

Someone loves you when they say you look wonderful, when in reality you look like a rotting old dog, with whiteheads the size of cockroaches.

? how does maturity affect rate of respiration in plants

My granny is 79 and her plants look glorious. Maturity definitely increases respiration in plants!

who's the best doctor who

I would like to help but will you give a idea on what kind of doctor you are looking for, I could better help with your question. Thank you.

what is the % change from 1.53 to 1.83

(*Applicant A*) I am not 100% sure what the % change from 1.53 to 1.83 is. 16 is the answer I am working out but I cannot confirm this, I do hope this helps somewhat.

(*Applicant B*) The sum has increased to 19,608%. That is what I came up with on this calculator. There are many calculators that do this.

how do you get from belgos to leicester sq station

To get from Belgos to Leicester Station: North End Rd to Finchley, to Brentmead Place. Take M1 to Leicester. then Wanlip Rd, turn left to Station Square.

? how many airports are there in the world

There are over 400 airports around the world, with most countries having at least one. The world's most busiest airport is believed to be in the USA.

? how do you say i love you in russian

To say 'I love you' in the native language – 'Russian' the correct pronunciation is as follows: Я тебя люблю.

? you make me feel, you make me feel, you make me feel

You make me feel like I want to run to the end of the road just to make sure I stay away from you as far as possible, because you stinks as a badger.

? is westwood ho worth visiting

Westwood Ho was worth visiting as it was famous for many years for cheap food and drink but it has already been closed on 17 November 2005.

how many times have spurs won the fa cup

Tottenham Hotspurs have won the FA Cup eight times. Their most recent FA Cup success was in 1991 where they faced still competition from Nottingham Forrest.

who will win wimbledon this year

The person who wins Wimbledon this year in the male section will be the one who wins all his games and the same goes for the female winner.

what is a good cryptic crossword clue for 'breakfast'

Good criptic crossword clues would be, 'It is the most important meal of the day' or 'It is the first meal of the day'.

? what was the best invention of the last millennium and why

The best invention of the last millennium was the lighting rod, invented by Benjamin Franklin in 1752, because it helps conduct electricity.

? who's going to win the fa cup

Judging by recent winners, the 07/08 season is likely to be won by Manchester United or it could be Arsenal, Liverpool or Chelsea.

? can i fly to portugal from luton

London Luton can take you to Portugal via Murcia, Alicante, Almeria, Madrid, Gerona, Barcelona, Reus, Malaga, and Gibralter. Have a good trip!

? **my teacher told me that the next person i meet will almost definitely have an above average number of arms: surely she's winding us up**

(*Applicant A*) When your teacher said 'an above average number of arms' she could have been referring to guns, so the next person you meet may own a lot of those!

(*Applicant B*) Your teacher must find you very huggable and believes you will meet someone who can appreciate you. Either that or she thinks you are artistic.

(*Applicant C*) Your teacher may be testing you with a logic question. Maybe she means coat of arms or another type of arm. Get some more info from her.

❓ send me a funny rhyming poem about my girlfriend: her name's tracey

(*Applicant A*) My girlfriend's name is Tracey, although it's fun, we must abstain, things are not always as they appear, while rocks boil with languid summer rain.

(*Applicant B*) There once was a princess named Tracey, It is rumoured she cried, Or at least, when she was spied, Over a prince all the way in Spain.

(*Applicant C*) Once met a lady named Tracy, her fella was a little hasty, she said 'like my new hat?' he said 'no you look fat' so she smacked him all over his facey.

❓ wow me with goat facts

Some Zimbabwean goat breeds can be trained in Kung-fu, to defend themselves against lions. Most goats can climb trees and all can see in the dark.

which supermarkets deliver to fishponds

Tescarp and Waitoads are both supermarkets well known to deliver to fishponds. For cheaper deals on your groceries, check in at your nearest Lidl-pad.

directions from malvern to basingstoke hospital

To get from Malvern to Basingstoke take a flight from Philadelphia Intl to Heathrow. Follow the M3 to get to Basingstoke. The hospital is on Elm Road.

can you still lose weight if you get a takeaway once a week

Takeaways have a lot of calories per meal. To lose weight if you are eating a takeaway once a week make sure you do not eat much else.

? **if you took all the £1 coins in circulation and stacked them up, would they reach right up into space**

> (*Applicant A*) As of December 2005, there were approximately 1,452 coins in circulation. They would not reach up into space if stacked up.
> (*Applicant B*) Yes, all of the £1 coins in circulation would reach space if stacked, as space is not far away at all, no matter where you go you are in space right now.

? **what's wrong with this sentence: i can't stand piano practice, however I can cope if it's tchaikovsky**

> The problem with the sentence 'I can't stand piano practice, however I can cope if it's Tchaikovsky' is that the work of Tchaikovsky is difficult.

❓ any fine women after me

The average man in his life will procreate with two fine women if you have had these two already then No!

❓ explain how the us elections work

The USA is run by squirrels. Each candidate is placed in a room with the bowl of nuts. The one to eat their nuts in the fastest time becomes president.